The Clown in the Gown Drives the Car with the Star

A BOOK ABOUT DIPHTHONGS AND R-CONTROLLED VOWELS

Brian P. Cleary

illustrations by
Jason Miskimins

Consultant:
Alice M. Maday

Ph.D. in Early Childhood Education with a Focus in Literacy
Assistant Professor, Retired
Department of Curriculum and Instruction
University of Minnesota

M Millbrook Press/Minneapolis

to Miss Gasper,
my seventh-grade teacher in Rocky River, Ohio
—B.P.C.

Millbrook Press
A division of Lerner Publishing Group, Inc.
241 First Avenue North
Minneapolis, MN 55401 U.S.A.

Website address: www.lernerbooks.com

Library of Congress Cataloging-in-Publication Data

Cleary, Brian P., 1959–
     The clown in the gown drives the car with the star : a book about diphthongs
and r-controlled vowels / by Brian P. Cleary ; illustrations by Jason Miskimins ;
consultant Alice M. Maday, Ph.D.
          p.   cm. — (Sounds like reading)
     ISBN 978–0–8225–7637–2 (lib. bdg. : alk. paper)
     1. English language—Vowels—Juvenile literature. 2. English language—
Consonants—Juvenile literature. 3. English language—Phonetics—Juvenile
literature. 4. Reading—Phonetic method—Juvenile literature. I. Miskimins,
Jason, ill. II. Maday, Alice M. III. Title.
PE1157.C543 2009
428.1—dc22   2008025477

Manufactured in the United States of America
1 2 3 4 5 6 – BP – 14 13 12 11 10 09

Dear Parents and Educators,

As a former adult literacy coach and the father of three children, I know that learning to read isn't always easy. That's why I developed **Sounds Like Reading**™—a series that uses a combination of devices to help children learn to read.

This book is the eighth in the **Sounds Like Reading**™ series. It uses rhyme, repetition, illustration, and phonics to introduce young readers to diphthongs—vowel sound combinations in which the sound of one letter glides into the other, as in t*oy*—and r-controlled vowels—vowels in which the sound changes because of the presence of the r, such as the *a* in *star*.

Starting on page 4, you'll see three rhyming words on each left-hand page. These words are part of the sentence on the facing page. They all feature a diphthong or an r-controlled vowel. As the book progresses, the sentences become more challenging. These sentences contain a "discovery" word—an extra rhyming word in addition to those that appear on the left. Toward the end of the book, the sentences contain two discovery words. And for an extra challenge, the final sentence in this book contains three! Children will delight in the increased confidence that finding and decoding the discovery words will bring. They'll also enjoy looking for the mouse that appears throughout the book. The mouse asks readers to look for words that sound alike.

The bridge to literacy is one of the most important we will ever cross. It is my hope that the **Sounds Like Reading**™ series will help young readers to hop, gallop, and skip from one side to the other!

Sincerely,

Brian P. Cleary

Look for me to help you find the words that sound alike!

oil

foil

soil

He poured **oil** on the **foil** on the **soil**.

saw

paw

jaw

I **saw** her **paw** on his **jaw**.

mouse

blouse

house

Can you find three words that sound alike?

The **mouse** took the **blouse** from her **house**.

herd

bird

third

Can you find three words that sound alike?

The **herd** and the **bird** finished **third**.

tar

car

star

Can you find three words that sound alike?

There is **tar** on the **car** in the shape of a **star**.

bow

mow

row

Can you find three words that sound alike?

The girl with the **bow** will **mow** grass in a **row**.

cow

plow

chow

The **cow** by the **plow** will eat her **chow now**.

clown

gown

crown

Can you find the word that sounds like clown, gown, and crown?

The **clown** in the **gown** has a **brown crown**.

Bert

skirt

shirt

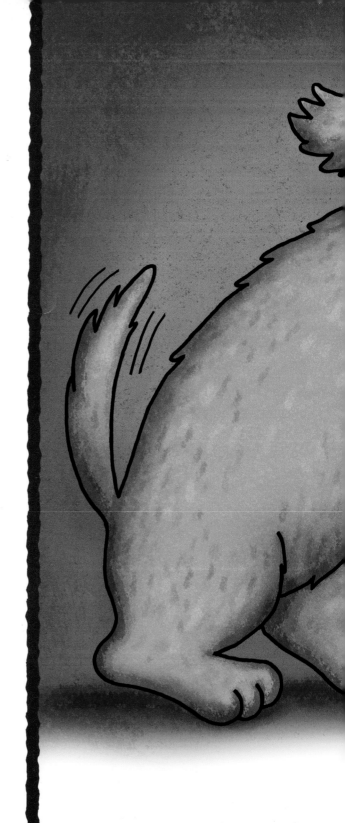

Can you find the word that sounds like Bert, skirt, and shirt?

Bert got **dirt** on her **skirt** and **shirt**.

squares

chairs

stairs

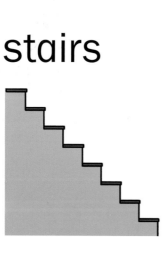

Can you find the word that sounds like squares, chairs, and stairs?

He **stares** at the **squares** on the **chairs** by the **stairs**.

crow

throw

snow

Can you find the word that sounds like crow, throw, and snow?

The **slow crow** can **throw snow**.

Troy

boy

toy

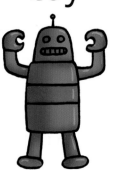

Joy and **Roy** gave **Troy** and his **boy** a **toy**.

scout

trout

spout

Can you find two words that sound like scout, trout, and spout?

The **scout** had to **shout** when he looked **out** and saw a **trout** with a **spout**.

cook

hook

book

The **cook** with the **hook took** a **look** at the **book** in his **nook**.

Brian P. Cleary is the author of the best-selling Words Are CATegorical® series as well as the Math Is CATegorical® and Adventures in Memory™ series. He has also written several picture books and poetry books. In addition to his work as a children's author and humorist, Mr. Cleary has been a tutor in an adult literacy program. He lives in Cleveland, Ohio.

Jason Miskimins grew up in Cincinnati, Ohio, and graduated from the Columbus College of Art & Design in 2003. He currently lives in North Olmsted, Ohio, where he works as an illustrator of books and greeting cards.

Alice M. Maday has a master's degree in early childhood education from Butler University in Indianapolis, Indiana, and a Ph.D. in early childhood education, with a focus in literacy, from the University of Minnesota in Minneapolis. Dr. Maday has taught at the college level as well as in elementary schools and preschools throughout the country. In addition, she has served as an emergent literacy educator for kindergarten and first-grade students in Germany for the U.S. Department of Defense. Her research interests include the kindergarten curriculum, emergent literacy, parent and teacher expectations, and the place of preschool in the reading readiness process.

For even more phonics fun, check out all eight SOUNDS LiKE READiNG™ titles listed on the back of this book!

And find activities, games, and more at www.brianpcleary.com.